DATE DUE		
DATE DUE		
JUN 22 2013		

SandCastle

Building Character

I Am a
Good Citizen

Mary Elizabeth Salzmann

Consulting Editor, Monica Marx, M.A./Reading Specialist

Published by SandCastle™, an imprint of ABDO Publishing Company, 4940 Viking Drive, Edina, Minnesota 55435.

Credits
Edited by: Pam Price
Curriculum Coordinator: Nancy Tuminelly
Cover and Interior Design and Production: Mighty Media
Photo Credits: Comstock, Digital Vision, Eyewire Images, Media Focus, PhotoDisc

Library of Congress Cataloging-in-Publication Data

Salzmann, Mary Elizabeth, 1968-
    I am a good citizen / Mary Elizabeth Salzmann.
      p. cm. -- (Building character)
    Includes index.
    Summary: Describes some of the many ways of being a good citizen, including following the rules, being friendly to others, and taking care of the Earth.
    ISBN 1-57765-825-6
      1. Citizenship--United States--Juvenile literature. [1. Citizenship. 2. Conduct of life.]
    I. Title.

JK1759 .S33 2002
323.6'0973--dc21

                                                                          2002066409

SandCastle™ books are created by a professional team of educators, reading specialists, and content developers around five essential components that include phonemic awareness, phonics, vocabulary, text comprehension, and fluency. All books are written, reviewed, and leveled for guided reading, early intervention reading, and Accelerated Reader® programs and designed for use in shared, guided, and independent reading and writing activities to support a balanced approach to literacy instruction.

Let Us Know

After reading the book, SandCastle would like you to tell us your stories about reading. What is your favorite page? Was there something hard that you needed help with? Share the ups and downs of learning to read. We want to hear from you! To get posted on the ABDO Publishing Company Web site, send us email at:

sandcastle@abdopub.com

SandCastle Level: Transitional

Your character is the kind of person you are.

You show your character in the things you say and do.

Good citizenship is part of your character.

I try to be a good citizen.

There are many ways to be a good citizen.

Good citizens follow the rules.

On the bus we stay in our seats.

We talk in quiet voices.

Good citizens are responsible.

When I check out library books, I bring them back on time.

I take good care of the books.

Good citizens are friendly.

At lunch I sit next to my friends.

I ask other children to sit next to me, too.

Good citizens are fair.

We let everyone play basketball with us.

Everyone gets to shoot the ball.

Good citizens take care of the Earth.

We pick up our trash.

We recycle paper, bottles, and cans.

Good citizens keep their yards looking nice.

I water the flowers in the garden.

Good citizens want to learn about other people and places.

Our teacher helps us find Japan on the globe.

What do you do to be a good citizen?

Index

Glossary

basketball   a sport played by two teams of five players that score points by throwing a ball through a high net

Earth   the planet that we all live on

garden   a place where people grow flowers, fruits, or vegetables

globe   a round model of Earth that shows the different continents, countries, and bodies of water

library   a place that has books, CDs, magazines, videos, and other materials that people can borrow

rules   instructions that tell you what you should and should not do

About SandCastle™

A professional team of educators, reading specialists, and content developers created the SandCastle™ series to support young readers as they develop reading skills and strategies and increase their general knowledge. The SandCastle™ series has four levels that correspond to early literacy development in young children. The levels are provided to help teachers and parents select the appropriate books for young readers.

Emerging Readers
(no flags)

Beginning Readers
(1 flag)

Transitional Readers
(2 flags)

Fluent Readers
(3 flags)

These levels are meant only as a guide. All levels are subject to change.

To see a complete list of SandCastle™ books and other nonfiction titles from ABDO Publishing Company, visit www.abdopub.com or contact us at:

4940 Viking Drive, Edina, Minnesota 55435 • 1-800-800-1312 • fax: 1-952-831-1632